www.finishinglinepress.com

When I Stopped Counting

poems

Charissa Menefee

Finishing Line Press
Georgetown, Kentucky

When I Stopped Counting

ACKNOWLEDGMENTS

"I Was Dragged into This Wilderness" and "Sounder Bite" originally appeared in
Amygdala.

"I am trying to remember when you remembered me" originally appeared in *The
2016 Hippocrates Prize Anthology*.

Publisher: Leah Maines

Editor: Christen Kincaid

Cover Art: Charissa Menefee

Author Photo: courtesy photo

Cover Design: Charissa Menefee

Printed in the USA on acid-free paper.
Order online: www.finishinglinepress.com
            also available on amazon.com

Author inquiries and mail orders:
Finishing Line Press
P. O. Box 1626
Georgetown, Kentucky 40324
U. S. A.

Table of Contents

This one is for my biggest fan, K.L.

And in memory of my great-grandmother, Sissy,
who gave me my first journal.

Shotgun

My father taught me
to fire a shotgun.
You had to have good aim
to shoot a pistol, he said,
so this offered better protection
for a girl of ten
babysitting her sisters,
even though the kick
might knock me down.

Dreadful

My hair is now so long,
so thick, that dreads form
when I'm not looking.
Rats' nests, my
grandmother called them,
and they used to actually
have rats in them, back
when wealthy women
wore towering wigs
adorned with flowers
and leaves and powder,
ships and dolls and
vermin.

She felt something
in her head—
an idea?!
No, just a mouse
tangled in neurons,
quietly scratching the
strands into cozy wads
where something
could live,
but never be seen,
never be heard.

An idea in a woman's
mind, hidden behind a
made-up face, hampered
by weighty fashion.
Stick out its little nose,
show it exists, and it will
surely be squashed.

Pinewood

In rural Tennessee, we ate
   squirrel and rabbit and frog legs
     because my father
           was out of work,

but I had my own room
   and a journal to write in,
     a unicorn beetle for my bug collection,
     and heard peacocks calling
           though I never saw them.

If It Was Monday, It Would Be My Birthday

You say it because it occurs to you, a fact
stated with no subtext, no hidden meaning,

because it is Friday and it is not your birthday.
But I may scream if one more person drops

by with an early birthday present, claiming to
always give before the actual day, be busy over

the weekend, or think the gift too perfect to wait.
They can't wait, but we do, still, hoping against

hope, to celebrate that birthday on Monday.
Because we know that someone is higher on the

list, someone not important to me, who'll see
his next birthday, who matters to his mother.

As my thoughts once again drift to the horrid—
accidents with donor cards but no survivors—

I know that I am weak, my heart stronger than
yours in measurable ways, but not in all the ways

it should be. Even so, I can't quite wish for
someone else to die so that my son can live.

If it was Monday, it would be your birthday,
and I would know you were all right.

But it is Friday, and this weekend
will not be long enough.

When I Stopped Counting

There was a year
     when the losses
kept adding up
     and once they
hit more than
     half a dozen,
before the
     spring equinox,
I had to
     stop counting.

Toto

I play Toto when I am five,
my role to follow Dorothy
everywhere and bark at everyone.

During a scene change, I get lost,
enveloped in red velvet, and find
myself in front of the curtain, facing
the audience, the yellow brick backstage.
No one knows I need glasses.

Dorothy burns her palms before the
final performance, but unwraps them,
exposing the red blisters, for the show.
So she can't hold me after she clicks
her red shoes, when the rope will lift
us up, up, up off the stage.

My dad says to hold tight to her
or I will fall instead of going
back to Kansas.

Some Things You Should Not Do

Keep your mother's headwraps and wigs and turbans, just in case

Believe you inherit everything

Forget your life is completely different

Ditched

Her father teaches her to drive,
in his emerald Buick,
on a little country road.

He says, *There's a ditch*
and there's a ditch—

stay out of them.

Her mother, from the back seat,
says, *Don't you need to tell*
her how fast to go?

She can go as fast as
she wants, he says,

as long as she stays out of the ditch.

I Was Dragged into This Wilderness

There is no map, so I navigate with
      suspect compass,
      half-baked advice,
      expert guesses.
In my dreams, I stroll out
      of the thicket,
      the sun blazing in front of me,
      this wilderness behind me.

Reading the Paper, Post 9/11

I devour the sports section
from front to back.

This makes sense.
This is reasonable.

This information
can be understood,
can be managed.

The simplicity of the
analysis, the expected
better-next-time refrains.

The profiles of determined
men and women—not
quite regular people—
but people you might know.

No frailty, no victims, no
unmonitored contests.
Surprises, but the kind that
bring delight, not fear.

Triumphs with rewards and
celebrations, not the kind that
leave destruction and death
and innocence in their wake.

In the days that follow,
as I discard other
sections of the newspaper

in favor of baseball scores,
pre-season football,
and basketball predictions,

I feel oddly informed.

I know some things for certain.

And they don't scare me.

In Defense of Nostalgia

You cannot rewrite my childhood
     as tainted,
     world-weary,
     long-suffered.

Who I am is based in that childhood;
     I won't have it
     traded in for a
     newer model

fraught with pop psychology and
     seeds of
     future
     dysfunction.

Crosswords

Artists do the crossword in pencil,
because they know that adjustments

have to be made for things to fit, that
words don't exist alone, in a void—

they work together, and sometimes
that means that the thing you

thought had to be, must be, right—
just doesn't work this time.

Ants

I.

They find me in the living room
chair, on the couch, in the bed.

Anywhere I am, they are.
I can never find where they get

in, can never track a solid line,
and they appear only when

I am nursing—or trying to
nurse—my newborn.

Emblematic of my failure, they come
for the sweet breast milk, which

seems to be everywhere except in this
apparently ever-shrinking baby.

II.

When I lift the lid off the candy dish
on the top shelf, I see wrappers, still

round in the middle and twisted on the
sides, but with only pockets of air inside.

Digging around, I find a wrapper with a
tiny ant in it, carrying a minute speck of

candy—sugar ants have dismantled each
lozenge, piece by piece, and stolen them.

How many hours, days, weeks, months
has this operation been going on, workers

slipping in through a sliver of air between
bowl and lid, sneaking into sealed packages?

III.

Why are the sugar ants here? So that I'll try
to get at least one more ounce of milk in this baby?

I can see, somewhere, a hill, astonishing in size,
made up of tiny mouthfuls of candy.

To a Young Mother

You are brave.
For how many eons have
women done what you do?
Not many—
it's different now.
You're expected to read
all the latest in parenting literature,
absorb media reports on child psychology,
in-womb exposure, pre-school preparation—
oh, but trust your instincts. Mold, shape, teach,
discipline your children, but only within the strict
guidelines approved by self-declared experts and
political pundits. Don't you dare think of mothering,
if you're allowed to say that rather than parenting,
as your primary contribution. You have to have
greater ambitions for yourself and your kids.
Their successes in career and celebrity,
however minor, will
excuse bad behavior,
lack of respect, selfish
indulgence, and inability
to see suffering around
them. Even if they cause
it. The media may tell
you that every mother's
dream is to have her son
buy her a house, but you
and I know how hard it is
to just raise good people.
You and I know we'd
rather hang out in a trailer
with someone we still like,
than live alone, forgotten, in a mansion.

My Parents Meet

She sits in the student union
with her date, a shy boy
from chemistry class;

my father sprawls onto the couch
opposite them, stretches his
cowboy-booted legs onto the
coffee table, and stares.

After the boy from chemistry
breaks into a sweat, excuses
himself for a moment,

my father tips back his black hat,
says, it's now or never, and she
takes his hand, because now
seems like a pretty good gamble.

It's Only Fifteen Minutes

How do
we expect

her to
go on

with her
life, when

the cameras
disappear and

the attention
fades—or

doesn't fade
quickly enough?

Barefoot

This is where a seamstress works every day,
so fabric, buttons, thread, bobbins, tissue-paper
patterns take up more space than people.

Straight pins and needles are always invisible
until I step right on them, but my feet—not
city kid tender—adapt to the risk and pain,

which seem no greater than honeybees in clover;
being barefoot is always worth it.

Marking the Pages

In the book
of your life,
I want to mark
the pages when
you were happy.
I won't tear out
the other pages;
they are part of
who you were.
But I don't want
to read them
again.

Even Though

An itinerant childhood meant no house was home,
each one a way station, a place we were visiting.

But home—the place that felt like the word
without claiming the name—

that would be my grandmother's house,
always my grandmother's house,

even though my grandfather lived there, too.

Sounder Bite

You know the way a story
deepens as you get further in,
the way the truth—
the complex and maybe hidden truth—
of a story emerges
during the actual telling?

How, if we're given time—
to explain,
voice concerns,
ask questions,
investigate reasons,
draw reasonable conclusions—

underlying motives,
unconscious fears,
stubborn hopes,
evidence of resilience
rise to the surface, and
we can experience
the difference between
hearing a sound bite and
learning someone's truth.

20/1500

I.
Surgery wouldn't just change my vision,
it would change the way I see.
Would I still be grateful that I live now,
in the twenty-first century,
when I am considered a sighted person?

II.
I labored all through the night, but when
the midwife called out for me to
look in the mirror, see my first baby's head,
I missed the chance to witness the birth.
My glasses were fogged up.

III.
In back labor with my third, I whipped the
glasses off, escaped into a world where I could
focus only on the intensity of the pain,
which felt as shapeless and blurry as the room
and the midwife's face.

Broken Pattern

We're the ones who broke it,
the pattern.
We got an education,
did not get pregnant
before we grew up ourselves.

But now our children's children
won't know their greats
the way we did—
the great-grandmas and great-grandpas,
great-aunts and great-uncles.

My children knew four
great-grandmothers
and two great-grandfathers.
Generations stretch out now.
That pattern broken, too.

My Grandmother Dreams She Is Sewing

Her wheelchair finally outside in the sun's warmth,
the memory returns to her arthritic fingers, the
needle's rhythm, the textures of cloth, buttons, thread.

My grandmother dreams she is sewing, the whirr
of the machine, pressing the pedal, feeding the fabric,
the stitches linking deftly as she turns the cloth at
precisely the right moment—a perfect corner.

I am trying to remember when you remembered me

for Peggy

I don't want to remember when
your eyes began to change—
how you knew me on Monday, but not on
Thursday, how the kindly nurses would
kindly explain that your kindly daughter
had come to visit, and how you would
nod on Wednesday, but shake your head
on Saturday and refuse to see me.

I don't want to remember when
you started telling me about your daughter,
the one with brown hair, the smart one,
the funny one, the one that was me.
She was young, with small children, so she
wasn't able to visit now, but she would
soon, and maybe I would like to meet her.

Charissa Menefee is a poet, playwright, director, and performer. She is on the faculty of the MFA Program in Creative Writing & Environment at Iowa State University, where she teaches scriptwriting, dramatic literature, and performance studies. A recent finalist for the Julie Harris Playwright Award, she has had plays honored by the Utah Shakespeare Festival's New American Playwrights Project, Pandora Festival of New Plays, and Tennessee Women's Theatre Project. She is co-founder of Tomorrow's Theatre Tonight, a reading and development series that introduced Arizona audiences to new plays for nine seasons, and was a Tennessee Williams Scholar at the Sewanee Writers' Conference. After spending many years in the mile-high mountain town of Prescott, Arizona, she now lives in Ames, Iowa.

www.ingramcontent.com/pod-product-compliance
Lightning Source LLC
LaVergne TN
LVHW021125080426
835510LV00021B/3323

9781635340297